This

Handwriting Practice

Joke book

belongs to

HOW TO USE THIS BOOK

1. Warm up by writing out some individual letters.

2. Choose a joke.

3. Write the date.

4. Trace the joke to help you remember it.

5. Write out the joke using the guidelines.

6. Make someone laugh by telling them your latest Halloween joke!

WARM-UP

Aa Aa Aa Bb Bb Bb

Cc Cc Cc Dd Dd Dd

Ee Ee Ee Ff Ff Ff

Gg Gg Gg Hh Hh Hh

Ii Ii Ii Jj Jj Jj

Kk Kk Kk Ll Ll Ll

Mm Mm Mm Nn Nn Nn

Oo Oo Oo Pp Pp Pp

Qq Qq Qq Rr Rr Rr

Ss Ss Ss Tt Tt Tt

Uu Uu Uu Vv Vv Vv

Ww Ww Ww Xx Xx Xx

Yy Yy Yy Zz Zz Zz

Joke #1

Date: _____

Why didn't the skeleton like the Halloween candy?
He didn't have the stomach for it.

TRACE THE JOKE:

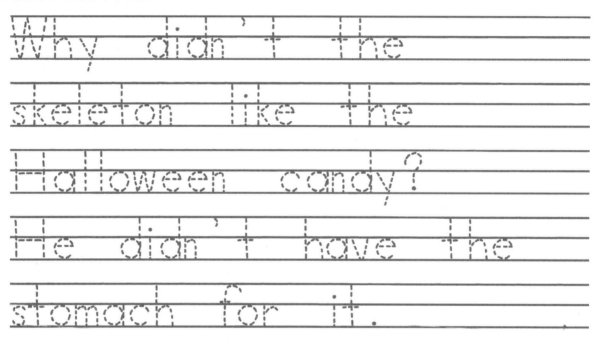

Why didn't the
skeleton like the
Halloween candy?
He didn't have the
stomach for it.

WRITE THE JOKE USING THE GUIDELINES TO HELP YOU:

✓ TELL SOMEONE THE JOKE! DID THEY LAUGH? ☐ ☐

Joke #2

Date: _____

Why do vampires use so much cough medicine?
To stop their coffin.

TRACE THE JOKE:

Why do vampires use
so much cough
medicine? To stop
their coffin.

WRITE THE JOKE USING THE GUIDELINES TO HELP YOU:

Joke #3

Date: _____

What do zombies like on their mashed potatoes?
Grave-y.

TRACE THE JOKE:

What do zombies like
on their mashed
potatoes? Grave-y.

WRITE THE JOKE USING THE GUIDELINES TO HELP YOU:

☑ **TELL SOMEONE THE JOKE! DID THEY LAUGH?** ☺ ☐ ☹ ☐

Joke #4

Date: _____

When is it bad luck to be followed by a black cat?
When you're a mouse.

TRACE THE JOKE:

When is it bad luck
to be followed by a
black cat?
When you're a mouse.

WRITE THE JOKE USING THE GUIDELINES TO HELP YOU:

 TELL SOMEONE THE JOKE! DID THEY LAUGH? ☐ ☐

Joke #5

Date: _____

Who plays the funniest jokes on April Fool's Day? Prankenstein.

TRACE THE JOKE:

Who plays the funniest
jokes on April Fool's
Day? Prankenstein

WRITE THE JOKE USING THE GUIDELINES TO HELP YOU:

TELL SOMEONE THE JOKE! DID THEY LAUGH?

Joke #6

Date: _____

> What's a ghost's favorite fruit?
> Booberries.

TRACE THE JOKE:

What's a ghost's
favorite fruit?
Booberries.

WRITE THE JOKE USING THE GUIDELINES TO HELP YOU:

Joke #7

Date: _____

What monster loves to dance?
The boogieman.

TRACE THE JOKE:

What monster loves to
dance? The boogieman.

WRITE THE JOKE USING THE GUIDELINES TO HELP YOU:

Joke #8

Date: _____

What do you call a pumpkin that has been dropped? A squash.

TRACE THE JOKE:

What do you call a
pumpkin that has been
dropped? A squash.

WRITE THE JOKE USING THE GUIDELINES TO HELP YOU:

☑ **TELL SOMEONE THE JOKE! DID THEY LAUGH?** ☐ ☐

Joke #9

Date: _____

What musical instrument do skeletons like playing most? The trom-bone.

TRACE THE JOKE:

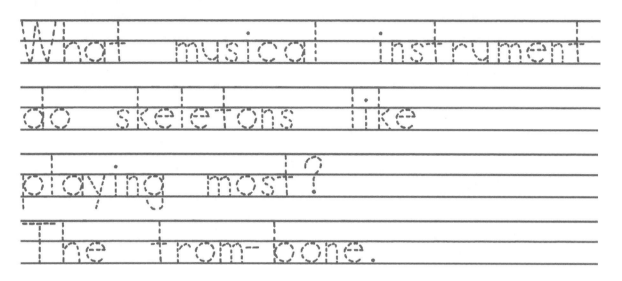

What musical instrument
do skeletons like
playing most?
The trom-bone.

WRITE THE JOKE USING THE GUIDELINES TO HELP YOU:

☑ TELL SOMEONE THE JOKE! DID THEY LAUGH?

Joke #10

Date: _____

Did you hear about the vampire who bit a snowman? He got frostbite.

TRACE THE JOKE:

Did you hear about
the vampire who bit a
snowman ?
He got frostbite.

WRITE THE JOKE USING THE GUIDELINES TO HELP YOU:

Joke #11

Date: _____

What do you call a monster who gets lost on Halloween? A where-wolf.

TRACE THE JOKE:

What do you call a
monster who gets lost
on Halloween?
A where-wolf.

WRITE THE JOKE USING THE GUIDELINES TO HELP YOU:

Joke #12

Date: _____

What is the most important subject at Witch School? Spelling.

TRACE THE JOKE:

What is the most
important subject at
Witch School?
Spelling.

WRITE THE JOKE USING THE GUIDELINES TO HELP YOU:

 TELL SOMEONE THE JOKE! DID THEY LAUGH?

Joke #13

Date: _____

What does a polite zombie say when it meets you for the first time? Pleased to eat you!

TRACE THE JOKE:

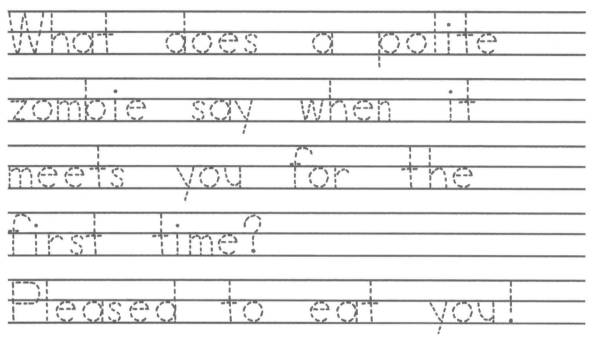

What does a polite
zombie say when it
meets you for the
first time?
Pleased to eat you!

WRITE THE JOKE USING THE GUIDELINES TO HELP YOU:

☑ **TELL SOMEONE THE JOKE! DID THEY LAUGH?** ☐ ☐

Joke #14

Date: _____

What do alien kids do at Halloween?
They dress up as humans.

TRACE THE JOKE:

What do alien kids do
at Halloween? They
dress up as humans.

WRITE THE JOKE USING THE GUIDELINES TO HELP YOU:

Joke #15

Date: _____

What kind of Halloween candy is never on time?
Choco-late.

TRACE THE JOKE:

What kind of
Halloween candy is
never on time?
Choco-late.

WRITE THE JOKE USING THE GUIDELINES TO HELP YOU:

TELL SOMEONE THE JOKE! DID THEY LAUGH?

Joke #16

Date: _____

What do ghosts eat on a hot day?
Homemade I scream.

TRACE THE JOKE:

What do ghosts eat
on a hot day?
Homemade I scream.

WRITE THE JOKE USING THE GUIDELINES TO HELP YOU:

☑ **TELL SOMEONE THE JOKE! DID THEY LAUGH?** ☺ ☐ ☹ ☐

Joke #17

Date: _____

Why did the monster bring toilet paper to the party? Because he was a party pooper.

TRACE THE JOKE:

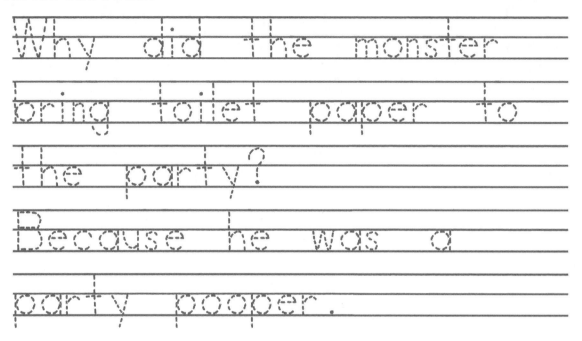

Why did the monster
bring toilet paper to
the party?
Because he was a
party pooper.

WRITE THE JOKE USING THE GUIDELINES TO HELP YOU:

☑ **TELL SOMEONE THE JOKE! DID THEY LAUGH?** ☐ ☐

Joke #18

Date: _____

What music do mummies listen to?
Wrap music.

TRACE THE JOKE:

What music do mummies
listen to? Wrap music.

WRITE THE JOKE USING THE GUIDELINES TO HELP YOU:

Joke #19

Date: _____

Why do pumpkins do badly in school?
Because they had all their brains scooped out.

TRACE THE JOKE:

Why do pumpkins do
badly in school?
Because they had all
their brains scooped
out.

WRITE THE JOKE USING THE GUIDELINES TO HELP YOU:

☑ TELL SOMEONE THE JOKE! DID THEY LAUGH? ☐ ☐

Joke #20

Date: _____

Why did the skeleton miss the party?
He had no body to go with.

TRACE THE JOKE:

Why did the skeleton
miss the party?
He had no body to
go with.

WRITE THE JOKE USING THE GUIDELINES TO HELP YOU:

 TELL SOMEONE THE JOKE! DID THEY LAUGH?

Joke #21

Date: _____

What does the vampire doctor say to his patients? Necks, please.

TRACE THE JOKE:

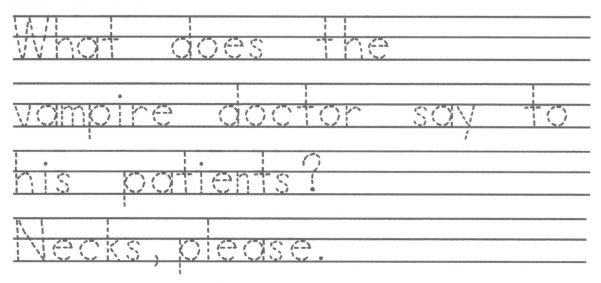

What does the
vampire doctor say to
his patients?
Necks, please.

WRITE THE JOKE USING THE GUIDELINES TO HELP YOU:

☑ **TELL SOMEONE THE JOKE! DID THEY LAUGH?**

Joke #22

Date: _____

What did the werewolf eat after having his teeth cleaned? His dentist.

TRACE THE JOKE:

What did the werewolf
eat after having his
teeth cleaned?
His dentist.

WRITE THE JOKE USING THE GUIDELINES TO HELP YOU:

Joke #23

Date: _____

What make-up do witches wear on Halloween?
Mas-scare-a.

TRACE THE JOKE:

What make-up do
witches wear on
Halloween?
Mas-scare-a.

WRITE THE JOKE USING THE GUIDELINES TO HELP YOU:

☑ **TELL SOMEONE THE JOKE! DID THEY LAUGH?**

Joke #24

Date: _____

What do zombies put in their chili?
Human beans.

TRACE THE JOKE:

What do zombies put
in their chili?
Human beans.

WRITE THE JOKE USING THE GUIDELINES TO HELP YOU:

 **TELL SOMEONE THE JOKE! DID THEY LAUGH?**

Joke #25

Date: _____

What do birds say on Halloween?
Trick or Tweet.

TRACE THE JOKE:

What do birds say on
Halloween?
Trick or Tweet.

WRITE THE JOKE USING THE GUIDELINES TO HELP YOU:

TELL SOMEONE THE JOKE! DID THEY LAUGH?

Joke #26

Date: _____

When do ghosts wake up?
In the moaning.

TRACE THE JOKE:

When do ghosts wake
up? In the moaning.

WRITE THE JOKE USING THE GUIDELINES TO HELP YOU:

☑ **TELL SOMEONE THE JOKE! DID THEY LAUGH?** ☐ ☐

Joke #27

Date: _____

What game do monster kids like to play at parties? Swallow the leader.

TRACE THE JOKE:

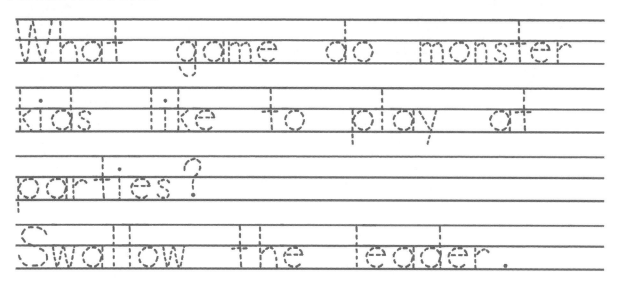

What game do monster
kids like to play at
parties?
Swallow the leader.

WRITE THE JOKE USING THE GUIDELINES TO HELP YOU:

☑ **TELL SOMEONE THE JOKE! DID THEY LAUGH?** ☺ ☹

Joke #28

Date: _____

How do you fix a cracked pumpkin?
With a pumpkin patch.

TRACE THE JOKE:

How do you fix a
cracked pumpkin?
With a pumpkin patch.

WRITE THE JOKE USING THE GUIDELINES TO HELP YOU:

☑ **TELL SOMEONE THE JOKE! DID THEY LAUGH?** ☺ ☐ ☹ ☐

Joke #29

Date: _____

Which is the heaviest monster around at Halloween? A skele-ton.

TRACE THE JOKE:

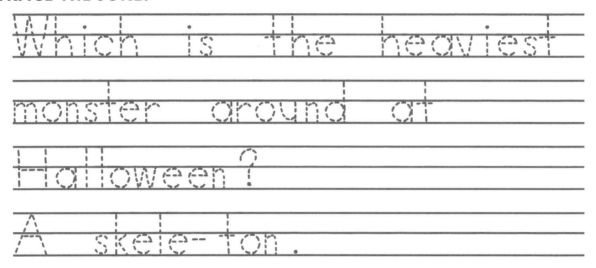

Which is the heaviest
monster around at
Halloween?
A skele-ton.

WRITE THE JOKE USING THE GUIDELINES TO HELP YOU:

_____

_____

_____

_____

_____

_____

_____

☑ **TELL SOMEONE THE JOKE! DID THEY LAUGH?** ☐ ☐

Joke #30

Date: _____

Why does Dracula not have any friends?
He's a pain in the neck

TRACE THE JOKE:

Why does Dracula not
have any friends?
He's a pain in the
neck.

WRITE THE JOKE USING THE GUIDELINES TO HELP YOU:

Joke #31

Date: _____

Where do werewolves store their Halloween candy? In a were-house.

TRACE THE JOKE:

Where do werewolves store their Halloween candy? In a were-house.

WRITE THE JOKE USING THE GUIDELINES TO HELP YOU:

Joke #32

What do you call a witch who loves going to the beach? A sandwitch.

TRACE THE JOKE:

What do you call a
witch who loves going
to the beach?
A sandwitch.

WRITE THE JOKE USING THE GUIDELINES TO HELP YOU:

☑ **TELL SOMEONE THE JOKE! DID THEY LAUGH?** ☺ ☐ ☹ ☐

Joke #33

Date: _____

What do zombies drive?
Monster trucks.

TRACE THE JOKE:

What do zombies
drive? Monster trucks.

WRITE THE JOKE USING THE GUIDELINES TO HELP YOU:

✓ **TELL SOMEONE THE JOKE! DID THEY LAUGH?** ☐ ☐

Joke #34

Date: _____

Which monster lives in Town Hall?
The Night Mayor.

TRACE THE JOKE:

Which monster lives in
Town Hall?
The Night Mayor.

WRITE THE JOKE USING THE GUIDELINES TO HELP YOU:

☑ **TELL SOMEONE THE JOKE! DID THEY LAUGH?** ☺ ☐ ☹ ☐

Joke #35

Date: _____

Which Halloween candy is the smelliest?
Footsie Rolls.

TRACE THE JOKE:

Which Halloween candy
is the smelliest?
Footsie Rolls.

WRITE THE JOKE USING THE GUIDELINES TO HELP YOU:

☑ **TELL SOMEONE THE JOKE! DID THEY LAUGH?**

Joke #36

Date: _____

Where do ghosts buy their Halloween candy?
At the ghost-ery store.

TRACE THE JOKE:

Where do ghosts buy
their Halloween candy?
At the ghost-ery
store.

WRITE THE JOKE USING THE GUIDELINES TO HELP YOU:

 TELL SOMEONE THE JOKE! DID THEY LAUGH? ☺ ☹

Joke #37

Date: _____

Why are graveyards so noisy?
Because of all the coffin.

TRACE THE JOKE:

Why are graveyards so
noisy?
Because of all the
coffin.

WRITE THE JOKE USING THE GUIDELINES TO HELP YOU:

Joke #38

Date: _____

What do monsters put on their ice cream sundaes? Whipped scream.

TRACE THE JOKE:

What do monsters put
on their ice cream
sundaes?
Whipped scream.

WRITE THE JOKE USING THE GUIDELINES TO HELP YOU:

Joke #39

Date: _____

Why do pumpkins sit on the porch at Halloween?
They have no hands to knock on the door.

TRACE THE JOKE:

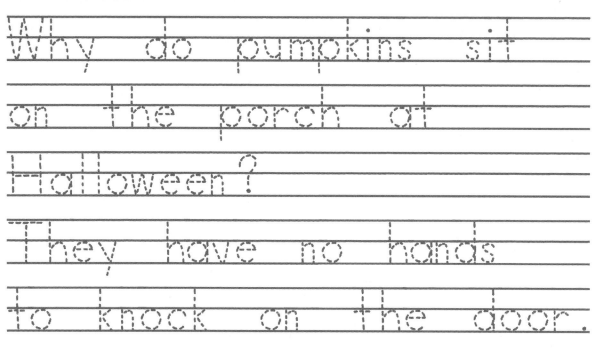

Why do pumpkins sit
on the porch at
Halloween?
They have no hands
to knock on the door.

WRITE THE JOKE USING THE GUIDELINES TO HELP YOU:

TELL SOMEONE THE JOKE! DID THEY LAUGH? ☐ ☐

Joke #40

Date: _____

Why did the skeleton stop going to school?
His heart wasn't in it.

TRACE THE JOKE:

Why did the skeleton
stop going to school?
His heart wasn't in
it.

WRITE THE JOKE USING THE GUIDELINES TO HELP YOU:

Joke #41

Date: _____

What is Dracula's favorite sport?
Bat-minton.

TRACE THE JOKE:

What is Dracula's
favorite sport?
Bat-minton.

WRITE THE JOKE USING THE GUIDELINES TO HELP YOU:

☑ **TELL SOMEONE THE JOKE! DID THEY LAUGH?** ☺ ☐ ☹ ☐

Joke #42

Date: _____

What holiday do werewolves celebrate in October? Howl-oween.

TRACE THE JOKE:

What holiday do
werewolves celebrate in
October? Howl-oween.

WRITE THE JOKE USING THE GUIDELINES TO HELP YOU:

 TELL SOMEONE THE JOKE! DID THEY LAUGH?

Joke #43

Date: _____

Why do witches have to wear name badges?
So they know which witch is which.

TRACE THE JOKE:

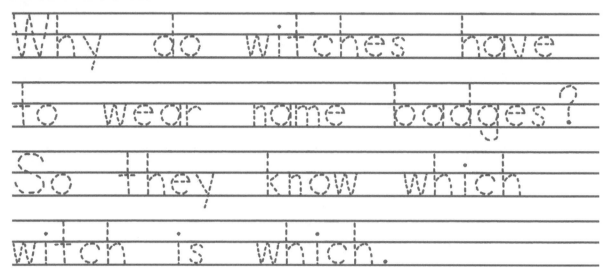

Why do witches have
to wear name badges?
So they know which
witch is which.

WRITE THE JOKE USING THE GUIDELINES TO HELP YOU:

☑ **TELL SOMEONE THE JOKE! DID THEY LAUGH?** ☐ ☐

Joke #44

Date: _____

What is every zombie's favorite toy?
A Deady bear.

TRACE THE JOKE:

What is every
zombie's favorite toy?
A Deady bear.

WRITE THE JOKE USING THE GUIDELINES TO HELP YOU:

☑ TELL SOMEONE THE JOKE! DID THEY LAUGH?

Joke #45

Date: _____

How do you spell candy using only 2 letters?
C-and-Y

TRACE THE JOKE:

How do you spell
candy using only 2
letters? C-and-Y

WRITE THE JOKE USING THE GUIDELINES TO HELP YOU:

☑ **TELL SOMEONE THE JOKE! DID THEY LAUGH?** ☐ ☐

Joke #46

Date: _____

Why did the ghost visit a hair salon?
To get a scarecut.

TRACE THE JOKE:

Why did the ghost
visit a hair salon?
To get a scarecut.

WRITE THE JOKE USING THE GUIDELINES TO HELP YOU:

☑ **TELL SOMEONE THE JOKE! DID THEY LAUGH?** ☺ ☐ ☹ ☐

Joke #47

Date: _____

How are haunted houses like libraries?
They're both full of horror stories.

TRACE THE JOKE:

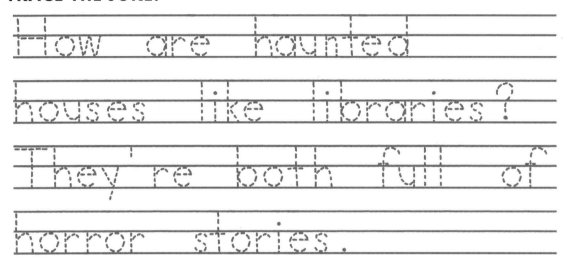

How are haunted
houses like libraries?
They're both full of
horror stories.

WRITE THE JOKE USING THE GUIDELINES TO HELP YOU:

✓ **TELL SOMEONE THE JOKE! DID THEY LAUGH?**

Joke #48

Date: _____

Do monsters eat popcorn with their fingers?
No, they eat the popcorn first, then they eat the
fingers.

TRACE THE JOKE:

Do monsters eat
popcorn with their
fingers? No, they eat
the popcorn first, then
they eat the fingers.

WRITE THE JOKE USING THE GUIDELINES TO HELP YOU:

☑ **TELL SOMEONE THE JOKE! DID THEY LAUGH?** ☺ ☐ ☹ ☐

Joke #49

Date: _____

Why couldn't the mummy get to the meeting?
She was all tied up.

TRACE THE JOKE:

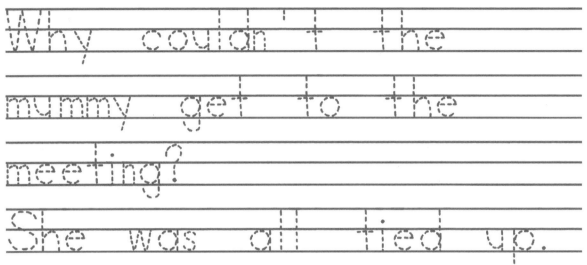

Why couldn't the
mummy get to the
meeting?
She was all tied up.

WRITE THE JOKE USING THE GUIDELINES TO HELP YOU:

☑ TELL SOMEONE THE JOKE! DID THEY LAUGH?

Joke #50

Date: _____

How come skeletons are so calm?
Nothing gets under their skin.

TRACE THE JOKE:

How come skeletons
are so calm? Nothing
gets under their skin.

WRITE THE JOKE USING THE GUIDELINES TO HELP YOU:

☑ **TELL SOMEONE THE JOKE! DID THEY LAUGH?**

Joke #51

Date: _____

What is the best vampire pet?
A bloodhound.

TRACE THE JOKE:

What   is   the   best

vampire   pet?

A   bloodhound.

WRITE THE JOKE USING THE GUIDELINES TO HELP YOU:

 TELL SOMEONE THE JOKE! DID THEY LAUGH?

Joke #52

Date: _____

What do you call a werewolf with a fever?
A hot dog.

TRACE THE JOKE:

What do you call a
werewolf with a fever?
A hot dog.

WRITE THE JOKE USING THE GUIDELINES TO HELP YOU:

☑ **TELL SOMEONE THE JOKE! DID THEY LAUGH?** ☺ ☐ ☹ ☐

Joke #53

Date: _____

How do witches tell the time?
They wear a witch watch.

TRACE THE JOKE:

How do witches tell
the time? They wear
a witch watch.

WRITE THE JOKE USING THE GUIDELINES TO HELP YOU:

 TELL SOMEONE THE JOKE! DID THEY LAUGH?

Joke #54

Date: _____

What Halloween candy should you give to a zombie? Life savers.

TRACE THE JOKE:

What Halloween candy
should you give to a
zombie? Life savers.

WRITE THE JOKE USING THE GUIDELINES TO HELP YOU:

✓ TELL SOMEONE THE JOKE! DID THEY LAUGH? ☐ ☐

Joke #55

Which monster won the Nobel prize?
FrankEinstein.

TRACE THE JOKE:

Which monster won the
Nobel prize?
FrankEinstein.

WRITE THE JOKE USING THE GUIDELINES TO HELP YOU:

☑ **TELL SOMEONE THE JOKE! DID THEY LAUGH?** ☺ ☐ ☹ ☐

Joke #56

Date: _____

Where do little ghosts go during the day?
Dayscare centers.

TRACE THE JOKE:

Where do little ghosts
go during the day?
Dayscare centers.

WRITE THE JOKE USING THE GUIDELINES TO HELP YOU:

✓ **TELL SOMEONE THE JOKE! DID THEY LAUGH?** ☺ ☐ ☹ ☐

Joke #57

Date: _____

Why don't door bells work in a haunted house?
They're afraid to make a sound.

TRACE THE JOKE:

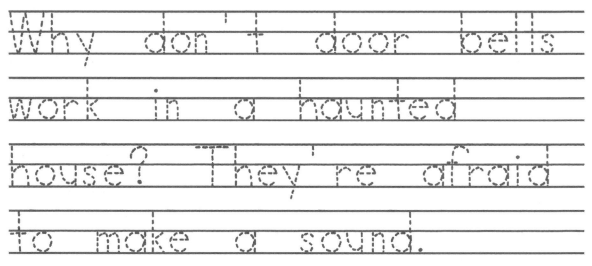

Why don't door bells
work in a haunted
house? They're afraid
to make a sound.

WRITE THE JOKE USING THE GUIDELINES TO HELP YOU:

☑ **TELL SOMEONE THE JOKE! DID THEY LAUGH?** ☺ ☹

Joke #58

Date: _____

What monsters have two mouths?
The ones with two heads.

TRACE THE JOKE:

What monsters have
two mouths? The ones
with two heads.

WRITE THE JOKE USING THE GUIDELINES TO HELP YOU:

☑ **TELL SOMEONE THE JOKE! DID THEY LAUGH?** ☺ ☐ ☹ ☐

Joke #59

Date: _____

What do skeletons say before dinner?
Bone appetit!

TRACE THE JOKE:

What do skeletons say
before dinner?
Bone appetit!

WRITE THE JOKE USING THE GUIDELINES TO HELP YOU:

 TELL SOMEONE THE JOKE! DID THEY LAUGH?

Joke #60

Date: _____

What is a vampire's favorite fruit?
Neck-tarine.

TRACE THE JOKE:

What is a vampire's
favorite fruit?
Neck-tarine.

WRITE THE JOKE USING THE GUIDELINES TO HELP YOU:

✓ **TELL SOMEONE THE JOKE! DID THEY LAUGH?** ☺ ☐ ☹ ☐

Joke #61

Date: _____

What do you get when you cross a werewolf with candy corn? A corn dog.

TRACE THE JOKE:

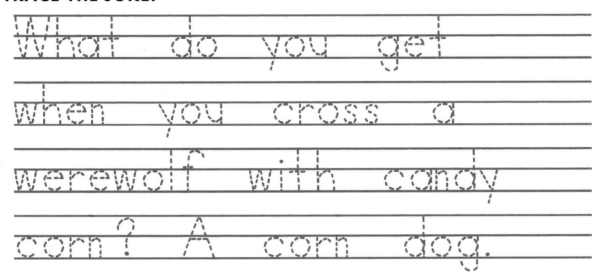

What do you get
when you cross a
werewolf with candy
corn? A corn dog.

WRITE THE JOKE USING THE GUIDELINES TO HELP YOU:

☑ **TELL SOMEONE THE JOKE! DID THEY LAUGH?** ☐ ☐

Joke #62

Date: _____

What has six legs and flies in the sky?
A witch on a broom with her cat.

TRACE THE JOKE:

What has six legs and
flies in the sky?
A witch on a broom
with her cat.

WRITE THE JOKE USING THE GUIDELINES TO HELP YOU:

✔ **TELL SOMEONE THE JOKE! DID THEY LAUGH?**

Joke #63

Date: _____

> What did the zombie do when he lost his hand?
> He went to the second hand store.

TRACE THE JOKE:

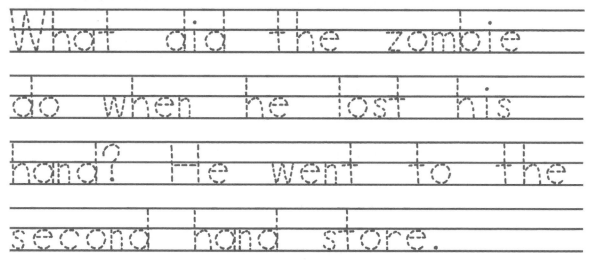

What did the zombie
do when he lost his
hand? He went to the
second hand store.

WRITE THE JOKE USING THE GUIDELINES TO HELP YOU:

☑ **TELL SOMEONE THE JOKE! DID THEY LAUGH?** ☺   ☹

Joke #64

Date: _____

Who taught the little candy corn how to play baseball? His popcorn.

TRACE THE JOKE:

Who taught the little
candy corn how to
play baseball?
His popcorn.

WRITE THE JOKE USING THE GUIDELINES TO HELP YOU:

TELL SOMEONE THE JOKE! DID THEY LAUGH?

Joke #65

Date: _____

Where do ghosts get their stamps?
At the ghost office.

TRACE THE JOKE:

Where do ghosts get
their stamps?
At the ghost office.

WRITE THE JOKE USING THE GUIDELINES TO HELP YOU:

✓ TELL SOMEONE THE JOKE! DID THEY LAUGH? ☺ ☐ ☹ ☐

Joke #66

Date: _____

What did Frankenstein's teacher say about his art project? "It's a monsterpiece."

TRACE THE JOKE:

What did Frankenstein's
teacher say about his
art project? "It's a
monsterpiece.

WRITE THE JOKE USING THE GUIDELINES TO HELP YOU:

☑ **TELL SOMEONE THE JOKE! DID THEY LAUGH?** ☺ ☐ ☹ ☐

Joke #67

Date: _____

What makes a skeleton laugh?
When something tickles his funny bone.

TRACE THE JOKE:

What makes a skeleton
laugh?
When something tickles
his funny bone.

WRITE THE JOKE USING THE GUIDELINES TO HELP YOU:

✅ **TELL SOMEONE THE JOKE! DID THEY LAUGH?**

Joke #68

Date: _____

Why do vampires use mouthwash?
Because they have bat breath.

TRACE THE JOKE:

Why do vampires use
mouthwash? Because
they have bat breath.

WRITE THE JOKE USING THE GUIDELINES TO HELP YOU:

☑ **TELL SOMEONE THE JOKE! DID THEY LAUGH?** ☺ ☐ ☹ ☐

Joke #69

Date: _____

Why was the werewolf angry with the skeleton?
He had a bone to pick with him.

TRACE THE JOKE:

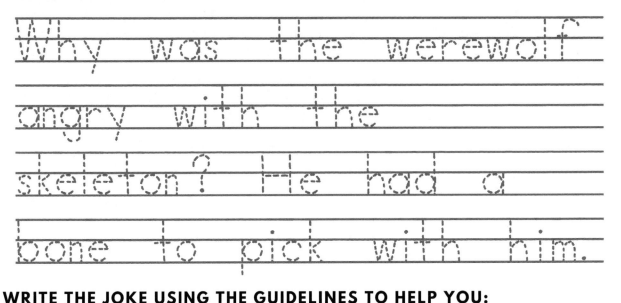

WRITE THE JOKE USING THE GUIDELINES TO HELP YOU:

☑ **TELL SOMEONE THE JOKE! DID THEY LAUGH?** ☺ ☐ ☹ ☐

Joke #70

Why couldn't the witch speak?
She had a frog in her throat.

TRACE THE JOKE:

Why couldn't the
witch speak? She had
a frog in her throat.

WRITE THE JOKE USING THE GUIDELINES TO HELP YOU:

✔ **TELL SOMEONE THE JOKE! DID THEY LAUGH?** ☺ ☐ ☹ ☐

Joke #71

Date: _____

What kind of bug will never die?
A zom-bee.

TRACE THE JOKE:

What kind of bug will never die? A zom-bee.

WRITE THE JOKE USING THE GUIDELINES TO HELP YOU:

TELL SOMEONE THE JOKE! DID THEY LAUGH? ☐ ☐

Joke #72

Date: _____

Why did the boy only want Mars bars at Halloween? He was dressed as an astronaut.

TRACE THE JOKE:

Why did the boy only
want Mars bars at
Halloween? He was
dressed as an astronaut.

WRITE THE JOKE USING THE GUIDELINES TO HELP YOU:

☑ **TELL SOMEONE THE JOKE! DID THEY LAUGH?** ☐ ☐

Joke #73

Date: _____

What happens if you give a black cat a lemon to eat? It becomes a sour-puss.

TRACE THE JOKE:

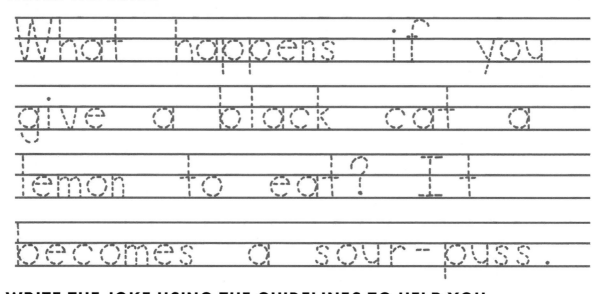

What happens if you
give a black cat a
lemon to eat? It
becomes a sour-puss.

WRITE THE JOKE USING THE GUIDELINES TO HELP YOU:

☑ **TELL SOMEONE THE JOKE! DID THEY LAUGH?** ☺ ☹

Joke #74

Date: _____

What bedtime story do baby ghosts like best?
Sleeping Boo-ty.

TRACE THE JOKE:

What bedtime story do
baby ghosts like best?
Sleeping Boo-ty.

WRITE THE JOKE USING THE GUIDELINES TO HELP YOU:

✔ **TELL SOMEONE THE JOKE! DID THEY LAUGH?** ☺ ☐ ☹ ☐

Joke #75

Date: _____

Where are the scariest haunted houses always located? At the end of dead-end streets.

TRACE THE JOKE:

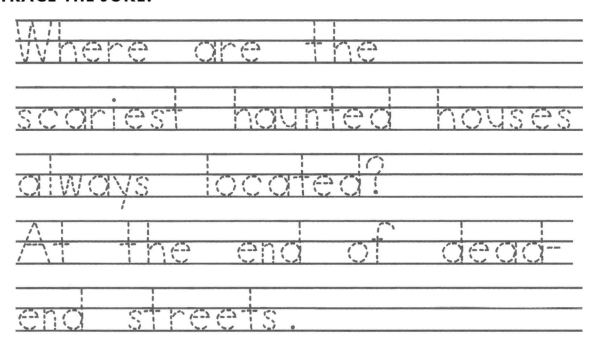

Where are the
scariest haunted houses
always located?
At the end of dead-
end streets.

WRITE THE JOKE USING THE GUIDELINES TO HELP YOU:

☑ **TELL SOMEONE THE JOKE! DID THEY LAUGH?** ☐ ☐

Joke #76

Date: _____

What do Italians eat on Halloween?
Spooketti.

TRACE THE JOKE:

What do Italians eat
on Halloween?
Spooketti.

WRITE THE JOKE USING THE GUIDELINES TO HELP YOU:

☑ **TELL SOMEONE THE JOKE! DID THEY LAUGH?** ☺ ☐ ☹ ☐

Joke #77

Date: _____

What is the best way to speak to a monster?
From very far away.

TRACE THE JOKE:

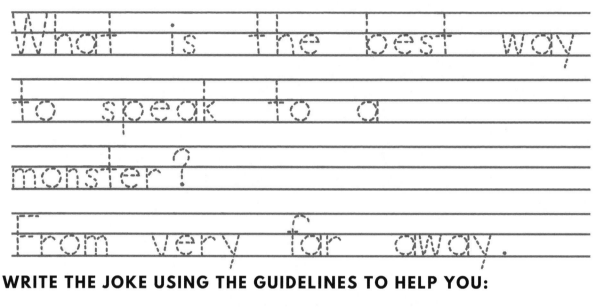

What is the best way
to speak to a
monster?

From very far away.

WRITE THE JOKE USING THE GUIDELINES TO HELP YOU:

Joke #78

Date: _____

What do you call a skeleton snake?
A rattler.

TRACE THE JOKE:

What do you call a
skeleton snake?
A rattler.

WRITE THE JOKE USING THE GUIDELINES TO HELP YOU:

TELL SOMEONE THE JOKE! DID THEY LAUGH? ☺ ☐ ☹ ☐

Joke #79

Date: _____

Why did the vampire go to prison?
He robbed the blood bank

TRACE THE JOKE:

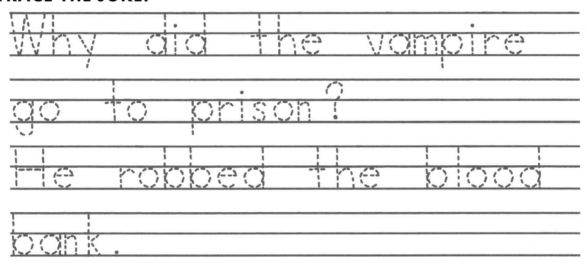

Why did the vampire
go to prison?
He robbed the blood
bank.

WRITE THE JOKE USING THE GUIDELINES TO HELP YOU:

☑ **TELL SOMEONE THE JOKE! DID THEY LAUGH?** ☐ ☐

Joke #80

Date: _____

Where is a werewolf's favorite place to hide?
In your claws-it.

TRACE THE JOKE:

Where is a werewolf's
favorite place to hide?
In your claws-it.

WRITE THE JOKE USING THE GUIDELINES TO HELP YOU:

☑ **TELL SOMEONE THE JOKE! DID THEY LAUGH?** ☺ ☐ ☹ ☐

Joke #81

Date: _____

What do witches get in hotels?
Broom service.

TRACE THE JOKE:

What do witches get
in hotels?
Broom service.

WRITE THE JOKE USING THE GUIDELINES TO HELP YOU:

☑ **TELL SOMEONE THE JOKE! DID THEY LAUGH?** 🙂 ☐ ☹ ☐

Joke #82

What do ghost teachers assign their students?
Moanwork

TRACE THE JOKE:

What do ghost
teachers assign their
students? Moanwork.

WRITE THE JOKE USING THE GUIDELINES TO HELP YOU:

☑ **TELL SOMEONE THE JOKE! DID THEY LAUGH?** ☺ ☐ ☹ ☐

Joke #83

Date: _____

What happened to the monster who ate his own house? He was homesick

TRACE THE JOKE:

What happened to the
monster who ate his
own house?
He was homesick.

WRITE THE JOKE USING THE GUIDELINES TO HELP YOU:

☑ **TELL SOMEONE THE JOKE! DID THEY LAUGH?** ☐ ☐

Joke #84

Date: _____

Which skeleton was a really famous detective?
Sherlock Bones.

TRACE THE JOKE:

Which skeleton was a
really famous
detective?
Sherlock Bones.

WRITE THE JOKE USING THE GUIDELINES TO HELP YOU:

TELL SOMEONE THE JOKE! DID THEY LAUGH? ☺ ☹

Joke #85

Date: _____

How did the vampire artist become so famous?
Because he was great at drawing blood.

TRACE THE JOKE:

How did the vampire
artist become so
famous?
Because he was great
at drawing blood.

WRITE THE JOKE USING THE GUIDELINES TO HELP YOU:

 TELL SOMEONE THE JOKE! DID THEY LAUGH?

Joke #86

Date: _____

What are werewolf kids' favorite bedtime stories? Hairy tails.

TRACE THE JOKE:

What are werewolf
kids' favorite bedtime
stories? Hairy tails.

WRITE THE JOKE USING THE GUIDELINES TO HELP YOU:

☑ **TELL SOMEONE THE JOKE! DID THEY LAUGH?** ☺ ☐ ☹ ☐

Joke #87

Date: _____

What jewelry do witches like wearing?
Charm bracelets.

TRACE THE JOKE:

What jewelry do
witches like wearing?
Charm bracelets.

WRITE THE JOKE USING THE GUIDELINES TO HELP YOU:

TELL SOMEONE THE JOKE! DID THEY LAUGH?

Joke #88

Date: _____

Why did the zombie stay home from school?
He felt rotten.

TRACE THE JOKE:

Why did the zombie
stay home from school?
He felt rotten.

WRITE THE JOKE USING THE GUIDELINES TO HELP YOU:

TELL SOMEONE THE JOKE! DID THEY LAUGH?

Joke #89

Date: _____

Why are ghosts always buying tissues?
Because they have a lot of boo-gers.

TRACE THE JOKE:

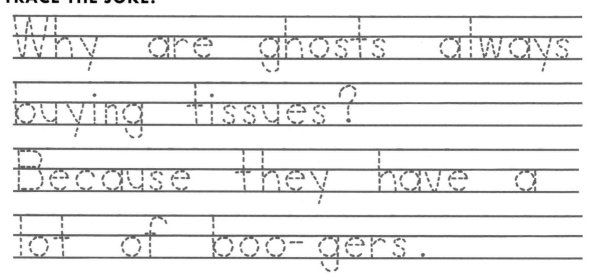

Why are ghosts always
buying tissues?
Because they have a
lot of boo-gers.

WRITE THE JOKE USING THE GUIDELINES TO HELP YOU:

☑ **TELL SOMEONE THE JOKE! DID THEY LAUGH?** ☺ ☹

Joke #90

Date: _____

Why did the headless horseman work hard at school? He wanted to get ahead in life.

TRACE THE JOKE:

Why did the headless
horseman work hard at
school? He wanted to
get ahead in life.

WRITE THE JOKE USING THE GUIDELINES TO HELP YOU:

✓ TELL SOMEONE THE JOKE! DID THEY LAUGH?

Joke #91

Date: _____

Why did the monster eat a light bulb?
Because he wanted a light snack

TRACE THE JOKE:

Why did the monster
eat a light bulb?
Because he wanted a
light snack.

WRITE THE JOKE USING THE GUIDELINES TO HELP YOU:

Joke #92

What did the skeleton order at the restaurant? Spare ribs.

TRACE THE JOKE:

What did the skeleton
order at the
restaurant?
Spare ribs.

WRITE THE JOKE USING THE GUIDELINES TO HELP YOU:

☑ **TELL SOMEONE THE JOKE! DID THEY LAUGH?** ☺ ☐ ☹ ☐

Joke #93

Date: _____

Did you hear about the vampire teacher?
She was always giving blood tests.

TRACE THE JOKE:

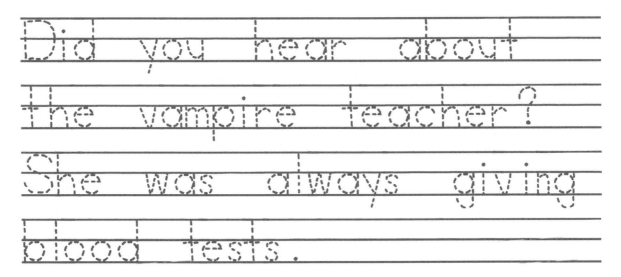

Did you hear about
the vampire teacher?
She was always giving
blood tests.

WRITE THE JOKE USING THE GUIDELINES TO HELP YOU:

☑ **TELL SOMEONE THE JOKE! DID THEY LAUGH?** ☐ ☐

Joke #94

Date: _____

What American city do werewolves gather in on Halloween? Howl-ywood.

TRACE THE JOKE:

What American city
do werewolves gather
in on Halloween?
Howl-ywood.

WRITE THE JOKE USING THE GUIDELINES TO HELP YOU:

TELL SOMEONE THE JOKE! DID THEY LAUGH?

Joke #95

Date: _____

What do you call two or more witches who live together? Broommates.

TRACE THE JOKE:

What do you call two
or more witches who
live together?
Broommates.

WRITE THE JOKE USING THE GUIDELINES TO HELP YOU:

☑ **TELL SOMEONE THE JOKE! DID THEY LAUGH?**

Joke #96

Date: _____

What happened when zombie chickens found a bag of gun powder? Egg-splosions.

TRACE THE JOKE:

What happened when
zombie chickens found
a bag of gun
powder? Egg-splosions.

WRITE THE JOKE USING THE GUIDELINES TO HELP YOU:

TELL SOMEONE THE JOKE! DID THEY LAUGH?

Joke #97

Date: _____

What's a ghost's favorite position in hockey? Ghoulie.

TRACE THE JOKE:

What's a ghost's favorite position in hockey? Ghoulie.

WRITE THE JOKE USING THE GUIDELINES TO HELP YOU:

☑ **TELL SOMEONE THE JOKE! DID THEY LAUGH?** ☺ ☐ ☹ ☐

Joke #98

Date: _____

What plants are most popular at Halloween?
Bam-boo.

TRACE THE JOKE:

What plants are most
popular at Halloween?
Bam-boo.

WRITE THE JOKE USING THE GUIDELINES TO HELP YOU:

TELL SOMEONE THE JOKE! DID THEY LAUGH?

Joke #99

Date: _____

Why was there no food left after the monster Halloween party? Everyone there was a goblin.

TRACE THE JOKE:

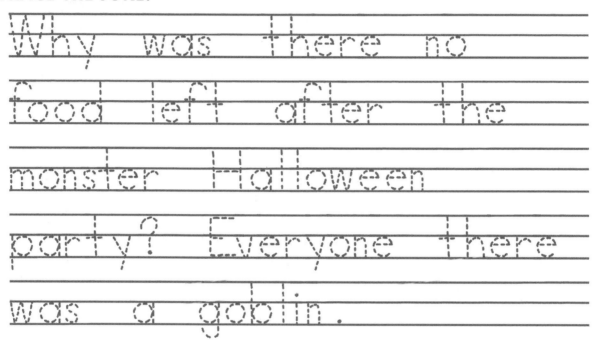

Why was there no
food left after the
monster Halloween
party? Everyone there
was a goblin.

WRITE THE JOKE USING THE GUIDELINES TO HELP YOU:

☑ **TELL SOMEONE THE JOKE! DID THEY LAUGH?**

Joke #100

Date: _____

Why don't skeletons play music in church?
Because they have no organs.

TRACE THE JOKE:

Why don't skeletons
play music in church?
Because they have no
organs.

WRITE THE JOKE USING THE GUIDELINES TO HELP YOU:

 TELL SOMEONE THE JOKE! DID THEY LAUGH?

Joke #101

Date: _____

What are vampires' favorite Halloween candy? Suckers.

TRACE THE JOKE:

What are vampires'
favorite Halloween
candy? Suckers.

WRITE THE JOKE USING THE GUIDELINES TO HELP YOU:

☑ **TELL SOMEONE THE JOKE! DID THEY LAUGH?** 😊 ☐ ☹ ☐

We hope you had fun learning some new jokes, and that you were able to make your friends and family laugh.

Happy Halloween!

Made in United States
Troutdale, OR
10/05/2024